The Uninvited

A Collection of True Life Supernatural and Paranormal Experiences

Paige Stone

Copyright © 2023 by Paige Stone

All rights reserved.

No portion of this book may be reproduced in any form without written permission from the publisher or author, except as permitted by U.S. copyright law.

Contents

Dedication		1
Foreword		2
1.	Chapter One: The Bedroom Window	5
2.	Chapter Two: The Basement Stairs	8
3.	Chapter Three: The Closet Door	10
4.	Chapter Four: The Melting Walls	14
5.	Chapter Five: Growling in the Attic	17
6.	Chapter Six: Voice at the Bedroom Window	20
7.	Chapter Seven: Basement Spirit	24
8.	Chapter Eight: The Forest Speaks	29
9.	Chapter Nine: The Candlelight Tour	33
10.	Chapter Ten: The Day Uncle Died	39
11.	Chapter Eleven: The Three Angels	41
12.	Chapter Twelve: Halloween Stranger	43

13.	Chapter Thirteen: The Closet Visitor	45
14.	Chapter Fourteen: And the Band Played On	50
15.	Chapter Fifteen: My Talk With Jesus	52
16.	Extra Content: The Curious Case of Mr. Black	55

Dedication

This is dedicated to my Mom.
For always encouraging my writing, being my best proofreader and for saving my life on numerous occasions.
Thank you for always being my biggest fan and cheerleader.

Foreword

The definition of "paranormal" is: "beyond the range of normal experience or scientific explanation; outside the possibilities defined by natural or scientific laws."

The definition of "supernatural" is: "of or relating to existence outside the normal world; attributed to a power that seems to violate or go beyond natural forces."

Supernatural and paranormal things take place all around us every day. You only have to be aware and perceptive enough to notice them. Many times, we try to explain these things away or seek a logical, reasonable or even scientific explanation for them. However, sometimes that's not possible.

In this world, there are certain people who possess the ability to have a connection with things that are supernatural or even paranormal. And, in some cases, certain people who were meant or designed to have a particular experience to start them on a journey of exploration to explain the unexplained.

I am one of those people. All my life, I have had experiences, both supernatural and paranormal. A couple of these experiences I share with you in this book took place when I was younger than 5 and are still so vivid, I can still remember as if they had happened yesterday.

There have been times in my life where I have had experiences or events happen on a daily basis. There was also a time in my life (from about 15-21 years old) where I shut it all out and refused to see the supernatural or recognize the paranormal. 25 years ago, there was not the popular talk and topics of ghost hunting, spirit seeking, mediumship, paranormal and supernatural that there is today. It was considered taboo and it simply was not talked about. And, in some opinions, is even considered demonic.

In my teenage years, I thought I was crazy because I knew no one else like me and had no one to talk to about my ability to see spirits daily and my mediumship. I am confident that if I had talked to anyone about it, they would have promptly locked me up in a very nice padded room, complete with matching straight-jacket, or tried to perform a rite of exorcism on me.

At the time, I didn't really understand the full extent of the gifts I had and why I have had experiences all throughout my entire life. I was also afraid that I, myself, was evil or demonic by having these abilities. So I tuned all of that out for a number of years because as if being a teenager and young adult isn't already hard and awkward enough.

It wasn't until I was a little bit older (early 20's) that I couldn't tune them out anymore. I was being bombarded with things daily I simply couldn't ignore. Like someone was telling me that I needed to embrace the gifts I was born with.

Instead of being afraid of my abilities, I took the time to learn about them. I was still having an internal battle of being a God-loving Christian woman who has mediumship abilities. Why should I be afraid of a talent or gift that has been given to me from God? My personal relationship with Jesus strengthened when I started to learn about my abilities more. He is my protection and He is my guide. There have been many times in my life where He has protected me from natural things, as well as supernatural and paranormal things.

In this book, I am going to share with you some of the things that I have experienced throughout my life. All of these events happened to me personally. Many of these experiences also included my mother, especially as a young child. Experiences that she remembers and reflects on, as I retell them.

Whether you are a skeptic in the paranormal and supernatural or are a hard-core believer with experiences of your own, it doesn't matter. I hope these events inspire you to find your own awareness of what is around you and in this world. There is more than you know and definitely more than you can see with the natural eye.

Chapter One: The Bedroom Window

When I was young, we lived in a nice part of town in Portland, OR in a townhouse type duplex. Growing up, I remember it was actually a very beautiful neighborhood. The complete opposite of what it is now and what has been seen on the news in recent years. Tree-lined streets, clean sidewalks, kept and manicured yards, super nice neighbors and rose gardens in the middle of every roundabout in each part of the neighborhood.

It's important to give you the layout of the house we lived in, as many of my experiences as a young child took place there.

The driveway to the garage went under the house, which was adjacent to the basement, and technically this was the ground floor. The main floor, which was technically the second floor, had the living room, kitchen, bathroom and one bedroom, which was my grandma's bedroom. The upstairs floor, which was the third floor, had a linen closet, my bedroom and my mom's bedroom.

We had a small but pretty backyard which was very private and mostly secluded. My bedroom was in the back of the house, overlooking the backyard, while my mother's bedroom that was just down the hall overlooked the driveway and the front of the house. I always had a hard time sleeping in my bedroom and I remember crawling into bed with my mom many nights as a child.

One night, when I was about four years old, I could not go to sleep. I felt like I was being watched. I kept getting goosebumps and was all tingly. Like the hairs on the back of my neck stood up and just never went back down. I felt uncomfortable, nervous and uneasy. I kept tossing and turning, trying to get comfortable, trying to ease this uneasiness. Even when I pulled my blankets over my head, I still couldn't escape the feeling I was being watched.

I rolled over (again, for the thousandth time that night) and faced my bedroom window. As soon as I rolled over, I screamed, jumped out of my bed and ran down the hall to my mom's room. She heard me scream and was coming to see what was wrong. I was so shocked by what I saw, I couldn't even tell her right away. I remember just hugging her, knowing I was safe.

Being almost 4 years old, it's not easy to communicate or convey things normally. However, I was articulate for being a little older than 4 and once I calmed down enough to catch my breath, I could finally tell my mom what happened. I explained to her that I had seen someone looking at me through my bedroom window. What I saw was a man watching me.

It was an older man, balding on top with wispy, thinning hair on the sides. He had old, sunken eyes, a very worn and weathered face, almost like leather, with very deep age lines carved into his face. All I saw was his head. No body or clothes or anything else. I finished telling my mom all this and I immediately asked her how he could get to my window because there were no ladders tall enough to reach. Like my little brain couldn't make it make sense as to how someone could have a ladder tall enough to reach my bedroom window.

My mom went down the hall to my room. She sat on my bed and looked over at the window. She looked out my bedroom window. She opened it and looked down. There was no one there and no evidence of a ladder. She even went downstairs and went outside to see if there were any marks in the grass from footprints or the base of a ladder. There were none. There was no indication anyone had been in the backyard at all. It would have been next to impossible to get to our backyard. They would have had to get through the neighbor's backyard first to get to ours.

This was one of my first paranormal experiences I can remember at almost 4 years old of a ghost man staring at me through my bedroom window. From that event on, I always feel like I am being watched no matter where I go. It is not something I have been able to escape.

Even now, over 40 years later, I can still remember that experience as if it just happened, with every detail of what the man looked like.

Chapter Two: The Basement Stairs

In the same house in Portland, OR, there was a set of stairs that led down to the basement from a door off the kitchen. In the basement, was our pantry, the laundry room, some storage and a connecting door to the garage.

One afternoon when I was about 4 years old, not long after the experience with the man watching me at my bedroom window, my mom went down to the basement to do some laundry. We had a golden retriever named Lady who followed my mom wherever she went. So naturally, Lady was down in the basement with my mom.

My mom told me I could sit at the top of the stairs while she started the laundry, since she was only going to be a few minutes and my grandma was not home at the time. So I did. I just sat at the top of the stairs with my feet on the next stair down, with my elbows on my knees and my head resting on my hands.

I did not get up. I did not stand up. I did not scoot closer off the top step. I did not lose my balance. I didn't even move. I was just sitting there, as I had done so many times before, patiently waiting to see my mom start coming up the steps, while listening to her sort the laundry & start the washing machine.

And then, suddenly and quickly, I was pushed from behind. I felt pressure on both my shoulders like a hard shove. I went headfirst down the stairs with no way to grab anything or stop myself. By the time my mom knew what was going on and heard the first tumble and hit the fourth or fifth step, Lady went and laid down at the bottom of the stairs and broke my fall.

The whole thing happened in less than five seconds. My dog basically caught me and kept me from hitting the cement floor at full speed. My mom ran over to Lady the second she caught me. I had no scratches or bruises and was completely physically unscathed. The only reason I was crying is because I was scared. I didn't know what happened or why I started to fall, since I did nothing to cause me to lose my balance.

My mom asked me what happened to make me fall and I told her something had pushed me. She asked me if I lost my balance or was sitting too close to the edge of the step and I told her no. We walked up the stairs together and I showed her exactly where I was sitting and how I was sitting. Again, no one else was home at the time, which is why she had me sit at the top of the stairs.

I asked her about this later on when I was older and she said there was no explanation as to how I fell down the stairs and that if Lady hadn't laid down at the foot of the stairs, I would've cracked my head open on the cement floor.

My beautiful dog, Lady, saved my life that day.

Chapter Three: The Closet Door

In my bedroom at the same house in Portland, OR, I had a very small closet. It wasn't a traditional clothes closet. It was more like a small coat closet, similar to what you would see in the entryway of a house. My bed was against the wall where the closet was, with my night stand on the other side of my bed.

The only things I kept in the closet were my coats, dresses and my shoes. Because my bedroom was small, the rest of my clothes were kept in a dresser in the bedroom downstairs where my grandma slept. I do remember there were things on the shelf above the rod, but I don't remember what those things were.

Starting about when I was 4 years old, I would hear knocking coming from the inside of my closet. It started out as one knock, almost like something inside the closet had just fallen over. Then it would be multiple light knocks. I told my mom I was hearing knocks coming from my bedroom. She explained the house was very old and it made noises sometimes.

I think it was about a month of the light knocking that had gone on sporadically, when the knocks seemed to get louder, a little more forceful and a little more regular. As a child, you try to rationalize situations with things you know. I thought maybe our cat, Henry, had snuck in my closet and couldn't get out. I thought maybe Henry had caught a mouse or a bird, brought it in the house and it found its way into my closet. And in the middle of that fear, your mind goes to the extreme, let your imagination run wild, until you realize that maybe there really are monsters living in your closet and under your bed.

I told my mom about the knocking noises from my closet and that I couldn't sleep. At first, she just checked things out to make sure there wasn't something broken in there and make sure there wasn't an animal in there. When the knocking continued, she cleaned out my closet completely. She took everything out, emptied the shelf and left it completely bare. She found no evidence of the cat, anything the cat could've brought in the house or any animal getting in there on its own, like a hole in the wall that a mouse could come through.

After she took everything out, I remember her opening the door to show me that there was nothing in there and the inside of the closet being blacker than black. The walls of the closet were painted white and there should have been some light shining into the closet from the light in the hallway, as well as from the light in my room. But there was none. It looked like an empty, black space — a giant void.

The closet was empty and my mom had proved it to me. It was quiet for a while. I don't remember exactly how long because when you are four years old, you have little to no concept of time. However, it didn't take long and the knocking started again. Just like before, it started softly at first and only once or twice a night. And again, the knocking increased in volume and quantity.

The house we lived in was built in the 1920s and was mostly the same structure; the same "bones". Only a few things had been updated or replaced over the years, but mostly cosmetic things. One of the things that was still original was the door knobs on all the doors, which included the door knob to my closet. They were all the same throughout the entire house. They were a gold colored metal base with a polished glass knob. When you touched it or turned it, it made a very distinctive sound, not like more modern door knobs.

And that's when I heard my door knob rattle. Something was trying to open my closet door. I know it was my closet door because my bedroom door was open. I was so scared to get up to run to my mom's room because I had to pass by the closet door to get out of my room and into the hallway. I was so afraid that whatever was making the noises in my closet was going to open the door and grab me. I just remember yelling for my mom at the top of my lungs.

I heard her open her door and rush down the hallway. As soon as she was one or two steps away from my bedroom, the rattling stopped. She sat down on my bed, hugged me and asked me what was wrong. I told her the door knob of my closet was rattling and wouldn't stop. I told her something was inside my closet trying to get out. She got up, opened the closet door and it was empty. There was nothing in there and she shut the door. But I didn't believe her. I insisted to her that there was something in there because I heard the door knob. I didn't want to look in the closet, but I wanted to show her what I heard. I leaned over the foot of my bed and reached around the corner to the door knob of the closet. I grabbed the door knob, turning it just enough to make noise, but not open the door. I moved the door knob back and forth to rattle it. It was the same unmistakable noise I heard and told my mom that the noises I just made with the door knob is exactly what I heard.

I did not want to stay in my room at all and asked my mom if I could come sleep with her. Of course, she said I could, but I didn't want to walk past the closet door. I asked my mom to stand in front of the closet door so I could walk behind her to get out of my room. I scooted behind her, past the closet door and out into the hallway as fast as I could. I remember that I did not go into my room and slept in my mom's room for over a week.

When I did finally choose to go back into my room, I remember being angry. Not angry that I had to go back to my own room, but angry that something scared me so bad. I remember the first time I walked down the hallway to my room and turned the corner, I kicked the closet door and yelled "NO!" at it. I continued to sleep in that bedroom for six more years until we moved and I never heard any knocking noises coming from it again.

Chapter Four: The Melting Walls

In my bedroom, in the house in Portland, OR, one entire wall of my room was bookshelves. My mom and grandma were both avid readers and collectors of books, you might say. Before I was born, my room was a catch-all storage room for things that needed frequent or regular access to and didn't need to go in the basement. This also meant storage for her books and my grandma's books, who lived with us at the time.

My room was pretty basic. It was the early 1980's. I had a bed, a night stand with a lamp and an alarm clock, a radio in the corner, a few boxes and a full wall of bookshelves. The bookshelves were directly opposite the wall of my bed.

Countless times throughout my childhood in that room, the bookshelves would appear to be distorted in a number of different ways. Sometimes they would look like they were very tall and skinny. Sometimes they would look like they were very short and fat. Other times, it would look like they were melting like lava or candle wax. A few times they would appear in normal shape and size, but looked like they were made out of something else, other than what they were made of. One time, they looked like they were made out of cement. One time, they looked like they were made of tree branches. Another time, it looked like they were made of glass. And one time, they looked like they were made out of black coal or black obsidian.

The first time I saw the bookshelves distort like this, I was about six years old and I thought I was dreaming about it. So I would just shut my eyes really hard & make it go away. The second time it happened, I took my fingers and pried open my eyes as wide as I could to make sure I was really seeing what I was seeing. The third time it happened, I pinched myself as hard as I could to make sure I wasn't dreaming. I pinched myself so hard, it left a bruise.

After proving to myself that I wasn't dreaming, I told my mom what was going on, what I was seeing, and showed her the bruise on my forearm. Each time it happened, I would pinch myself on my arm or my leg to assure my brain that what I was seeing was real. And each time, tell my mom that it happened again and show her the bruise I made. This must have happened close to twenty times.

One night, the shelves appeared to be melting and on fire. There was no heat coming from the fire and nothing else in my room was melting or distorted. In the middle of the fire was a black circle that had never been there before. The black circle grew and grew and in a very short amount of time, it became the size of a hula hoop, with flames all around it and the edges melting like wax. I could not see anything in the black circle, but I could hear voices.

The voices were saying things like,

"We must take her."

"Come with us."

"Step through the circle."

"The flames won't hurt you."
"You belong with us."

They were soft, wispy voices. Very airy, breathy voices, repeating these over and over, talking over each other, beckoning me, calling to me to come to the black circle.

I screamed as loud as I could because it was the only thing I could do. I was afraid to move to turn on the ceiling light. I was afraid to get off my bed & run, that I could somehow be grabbed and dragged into that circle. I was absolutely frozen with fear.

My mom ran into my room and turned the light on. Instantly the black circle and the flames were gone, fully extinguished, the bookcase restored to normal. My mom asked me what made me scream and I told her exactly what happened – what I saw and what I heard. From that night on, I slept with the ceiling light on in that bedroom. I never wanted it dark in my room or even dim, where anything could cast shadows.

At the time, we were practicing Roman Catholics and she had our priest come bless our house. After that, I never experienced the bookshelves getting distorted again. When I got older, I asked my mom about those experiences with that. She said that the priest basically did an exorcism on our house and that she believes that, had I gotten close to the circle or actually listened to the voices, I would have or could have been demonically possessed. She said both her and our priest believed that what I saw was a portal to hell.

From that day forward, I have always had a deep connection, a deep relationship with Jesus. I literally saw hell that night and knew that's not anything I wanted to be associated with or ever see again.

Chapter Five: Growling in the Attic

In our house in Portland, at the first stair landing leading up to the 3rd floor and my bedroom, there was a small square door on the side of the wall. This was the door to our attic. The attic itself wasn't very big and neither was the door. As a child, it seemed huge. But now as an adult remembering back to it, the door was probably 2 ½ - 3 feet by 2 ½ - 3 feet square. The size of the attic itself was maybe 4 feet by 4 feet, maybe at the most 5 feet by 5 feet. I don't remember if there was a ton of stuff stored in the attic and only remember seeing the attic door open a handful of times, even though I passed by it multiple times a day.

The door was on the wall and opened like a traditional door, rather than a normal attic door that opens downward and has a ladder to go up into it. The attic was already at one of the highest points of the house, so there was no need for a ladder. There was no light inside the attic and we could only see inside with a flashlight.

One time when I was about seven, my mom was clearing out the attic to go through the things that had been in there and ultimately anything that was being kept, would be moved to the storage area in the basement. While she was doing this, I was curious about what was in the attic, since I had only seen the door open a couple of times before. I helped her by holding the flashlight, while she would pull out boxes and take them downstairs to the living room to sort through things.

My mom had taken a box downstairs and I was still holding the flashlight with the attic door open. I shined the light into the dark, black attic, just to see what it looked like. As I shone the light in the attic, I didn't see anything except the couple of boxes that were left. I thought it was a weird space to put boxes and as a kid it didn't make sense to me.

So I took the flashlight and looked around, standing on the landing next to the attic door. I was not doing anything inside the attic or even looking inside the attic, but the attic door was still open. I heard this low rumble in my left ear, which is the side the attic door was on to where I stood. I shined the flashlight inside the door and didn't see anything different from what I saw before. I checked to see if maybe our cat, Henry, had somehow managed to get in the attic and was growling at something other than me. But I had been standing there the whole time and didn't see Henry once. I also remember thinking maybe we were going to have a thunder and lightning storm because I love thunder and lightning. I yelled down the stairs to my mom if she heard the thunder. She said no she didn't hear anything and I thought it was maybe just because I was closer to the roof that I could hear it and she couldn't.

Then I heard something again, but it wasn't a low rumble. It sounded like a low growl, like something our golden retriever, Lady, or a dog in general would make. I looked around to see if Lady was laying in the hallway between my mom's bedroom and mine. She was not. Since my mom's bedroom was closest to where I was, I went up the rest of the stairs to see if Lady was in her room. She was not. I went back to the stair landing and yelled to my mom, asking if Lady was downstairs with her. She said she was. My little brain could not understand this noise, where it was coming from and what it was.

My mom came back up the stairs to grab another box out of the attic. I got my flashlight ready for her and shined it in the attic. This time when I shined it inside, the flashlight wasn't as bright. It was very dim and the attic looked darker inside, if that was possible. My mom grabbed the next box and went back downstairs. As soon I heard her set the box down, a low, deep, guttural growl came from inside the attic. This sound was different from any other sound I had heard. This growl was mean, vicious and dangerous.

I slammed the attic door shut, ran down the stairs to where my mom was and told her about the noises I heard. I explained what they sounded like and why I asked her about the thunder and where Lady was. I told her about the last sound I heard and that I didn't want to help her anymore because it was scary. She said she only had two more boxes to get out of there and if I could help her by holding the flashlight to get them out, we would be done. So we walked up the stairs together, she opened the attic door, I shined the flashlight inside (hands shaking), she grabbed the box and I slammed the door shut to follow her back downstairs.

We did that exact sequence one more time to get the last box and the attic door was never opened again for as long as we lived there. I never heard that sound from the attic again.

Chapter Six: Voice at the Bedroom Window

In our house in Portland, my mom's bedroom was technically on the third floor. One set of windows overlooked the side yard between our house and our neighbor's house. The other window had a perched sitting area or small window seat that overlooked the front of the house, where the trees and the driveway were.

At eye level with the window was the top ¼ of the trees and it was beautiful to sit there and see nothing but the trees. It was especially beautiful when it was snowing because there was nothing "city" or any structures obscuring or interfering with your view of the trees. With all the experiences I had in this house as a kid, I loved sitting at this window and reading. Not only was my mom's room my place to go when I was scared, but it was my safe place no matter what.

When I was about seven years old, I was sitting on the seat below the window. My mom was folding laundry while we were watching something on TV. I was just watching the TV show kind of snuggled up in a blanket. I stood up on the seat to rearrange my blanket and noticed that I was finally tall enough to look out the window and look straight down to the driveway, three stories below.

I am severely afraid of heights, so it was a little dizzying to look out the window, straight down to the driveway. I was scared, yet a little fascinated that I could look down and know I couldn't fall. I think the fear of suddenly falling is most of what makes up my fear of heights. Not only could I still watch just the trees, but now I could see the whole street, the whole neighborhood. It was like an entirely new set of lenses for me.

Each time I was in my mom's room from that point on, I would climb up on the window seat to look out over the neighborhood. Had anything changed since the last time I looked? What was going on outside the four walls of our house? It was fun to see the leaves changing in the fall and see all the multi-colored leaves on the ground. In the fall, you could see the gray, stormy skies, the changing leaves, the rain falling and the wet pavement all in one glance. It was also the perfect place to watch a thunder and lightning storm. You could see the bolts of lightning streak across the sky behind the tree branches.

One gray, stormy Sunday in the fall, I was watching TV with my mom in her room. She was sitting in a padded chair and I was sitting on the window seat. She got up to go downstairs to the bathroom. I stood up on the window seat to look out the window. I think I used this as a way to try to get over my fear of heights. I thought that looking straight down from three stories up and trying to build up a tolerance to heights would cure or desensitize me of my fear.

So I stood on the window seat looking down at where the edge of the driveway met the edge of the sidewalk.

A voice said, "*Open the window.*"

It was like a quiet whisper in my ear. I had only seen that window open once that I could remember. I wasn't sure it would open or if I could open it, even if I wanted it to.

"*Open the window.*" it said again.

I remember being kind of mesmerized by this voice. It was soft, wispy, kind, gentle and inviting. Almost sing-song like. I looked around for the latch to open the window. This window opened differently than every other window in the rest of the house. All the other windows had a latch at the top and slid upwards. This window had a latch at the top, in the middle of two window panes that split and opened inward. There was a screen on the window, so I still felt like I was safe from falling and my fear of heights.

"*Why don't you sit on the window sill?*" the voice said.

The window sill was only about five inches deep and there wasn't much room for me to sit. But I thought I could at least get my knees on it. So I get one knee up on the window sill, while holding onto the windows. Just as I was about to put the other knee up on the window sill, where the full weight of my body would have been balancing on the sill and leaning against the screen, my mom walked back in the room and saw what I was doing.

I had never seen her move so fast, as she moved from the doorway of the room, across the room to the room to the window. She scooped me off that window sill and set me down on her bed. She immediately closed the window and latched it shut. She was frantic and asked me what I was doing. I told her about the voice that I heard that was so nice, inviting, telling me to open the window and then asking me to sit on the window sill. She explained to me what would've most likely happened, with me falling through the screen and falling three stories to the cement below. She explained that I would most likely be dead.

I hadn't even realized that what I was doing, or rather being influenced to do, would have caused me any harm. And not even because of how old I was, but that in those moments, I had no fear of something I had always been deathly afraid of and the verbal requests from something I couldn't see. Once my mom explained to me what could have happened, it terrified me that I could have done anything like that. I am so thankful that she came back into the room when she did. She literally saved my life. Again.

Chapter Seven: Basement Spirit

My best friend growing up had the coolest house, in the coolest location. Their house was a single story house with a full basement, seated in the middle of about 5 acres of trees. It had the biggest kitchen I'd ever seen with a large picture window that faced the driveway and the very large front yard. We spent a fair amount of time in that kitchen making cookies and doing art projects as kids, and we'd help make dinner and snacks. Their driveway was about a quarter-mile long through a forest that opened into a clearing where the house stood. Their entire property was probably about seven acres, with an immense garden in the backyard and a sloped hill behind the garden area, which led to a creek running directly behind the property. I loved everything about this house and this property because it was so quiet, full of nature and there was so much for us kids to do- inside and outside.

All the main parts of the house were on the main floor. Down in the basement was the pantry, a full second living room or family room area, a small office area with a desk and a filing cabinet, the laundry room, an unfinished bedroom, a bathroom and some small storage. There were windows near the ceiling of every room in the basement. It wasn't quite a daylight basement, but the basement was built high enough under the house where there was natural light anywhere you went.

When I would spend the night, we would basically have a slumber party down in the basement. It had furniture with a foldout couch, a TV, a VCR (yes, it was the 80s), a stereo and lots of room to run around, play, have fun and be kids. It was the complete opposite of the basement at our house.

Sometimes it was just me spending the night and other times, a couple of our other friends stayed too. Then it really was a true slumber party. We could be loud (ish) and not bother her parents (too much). We could watch movies, have snacks and play games. It was always a lot of fun.

One Saturday, when we were all about eight years old, we had one of these slumber parties. There were four of us at that time. During the day, we played outside, went down to the creek, made cookies and I remember just having a great day that day.

Whenever there were a bunch of us staying over, we'd always rent movies to watch or play games down in the basement. This particular night, one of our friends brought a Ouija board. We all thought it was cool because the only person who had used it before was the person who brought it. None of us had any clue what it was and what it could do.

Our friend started by explaining to us that we use the marker (the planchet) to talk to ghosts using the letters and the answers on the board. We asked her what kind of ghosts we could talk to. She told us we could talk to any ghost we wanted. We all thought this was something really cool and we couldn't wait to see what happened. Since none of us knew what to do or how to use it, except our one friend, she kind of led "the game". And that's kind of what we all thought it was, was a game.

We sat on the floor of the downstairs family room and started "the game" with all 4 of us sitting around the board. Our friend explained that any of us could have our hands on the marker at the same time and that we ask whatever questions we want to, then the answers would either be answered using the "Yes", the "No" or spell out words. She explained that we don't move the marker, but that the ghost who is talking to us will move it and that we just keep our hands on the marker to know it's real.

She started out by asking if there were any ghosts or spirits with us that wanted to talk to us. We waited for maybe twenty seconds and the marker started moving. It was moving toward one of our friends and the friend sitting opposite her told her to stop moving the marker. She said she wasn't moving it and thought the other friend was moving it. We all took our hands off the planchet and it stayed still. The two girls were getting irritated with each other, saying the other one moved it on purpose to scare them.

Our friend, who brought the board, told each of us to put one finger lightly on the marker so we don't accidentally move it. We all, one by one, put one finger on the planchet and she asked again if there were any ghosts or spirits with us that wanted to talk to us. I'm pretty sure we all held our breath, not trying to move the planchet, waiting for any sign of movement. About fifteen seconds after she asked the question, the marker began moving again. It moved down towards the bottom of the board and then swung up slowly towards "Yes". It moved away from "Yes" and then back over it again.

This was kind of exciting. We were talking to a ghost or spirit who wanted to talk to us. Our friend asked the ghost if it could say "Hello" to us. The marker moved away from "Yes", closer to "No", then moved down the board slowly to "H". Then to "I". It spelled out "Hi". Like our little 8-year-old minds were blown that we were having a conversation with a ghost! It was exciting and scary at the same time. It was smart and intelligent and had answered our question.

We were all trying to figure out what to ask next. I piped up and said we should ask its name. So our friend, who was leading "the game" asked if it could tell us its name. The planchet didn't move for probably close to a minute. Then it went to "S", slowly to "O", back around to "S" and again to "O". It spelled out So-So. For an 8-year-old brain, so-so meant that you were kind of okay or maybe it didn't understand the question or we thought maybe it was shy and wanted to give us its name, but didn't want to at the same time. Like there was nothing scary or bad about this name. There was nothing bad or scary that we felt or experienced.

For the next fifteen minutes, we asked a variety of questions like, "Are you a boy or a girl?", "How old were you when you died?", "Did you live near here?" Questions like that. We received straight up basic answers for everything we asked, moving the planchet to either "Yes" or "No". Up to this point, the only thing it spelled out was the answer it gave when we asked its name.

Then our one friend asked "Are you good or bad?" The planchet flew across the board to "No". She told the spirit that "No" wasn't an answer to her question and she asked the same question again. We were all anxious about the answer we were going to get. We kept our one fingers on the planchet as lightly as we could, waiting for it to move, but terrified that it would actually move. It moved the slowest it had moved all night. First to "B". One girl took her finger off the marker. Next to "A". Another girl took her finger off the marker, leaving only two of us touching it. Then to "D". We both took our fingers off the planchet like it had shocked us or was poison and it flew up to "No", just hovering there, vibrating back and forth.

Our friend that brought the Ouija board suddenly yelled out "Stop!!" In that instant, the planchet stopped vibrating, stopping all movement. She put the board and the planchet back in the box, ran upstairs and put the box with all its contents in the front yard and left it. We waited, holding our breath, for her to come back downstairs. Once she did, we all four huddled on the fold out bed, freaked out of our minds for the rest of the night. We stayed up all night watching movies, so as to distract us from the experience we all had. None of us slept at all that night. This was the first and last time I ever used a Ouija board.

As I got older and studied spirits, entities, the paranormal and the supernatural, I ran across a name almost identical to So-So. I was gob smacked. I was so shocked at what I learned and at the same time so blessed and thankful that something extremely evil did not happen to any of us. For those of you who do not know, the name of one of the most evil demon spirits is ZoZo. ZoZo likes to come through using Ouija boards and other means of paranormal tools, disguised as some other type of spirit. It can be inviting and has the ability to hurt you, harm you or possess you.

Chapter Eight: The Forest Speaks

I spent a lot of time at the same friend's house where we had the Ouija board experience. I loved her house. The driveway was like a ¼ mile long that was surrounded by forest trees. The closer you got to the house, the forest opened up into a greenspace lawn. It was like the house and property was surrounded by its own natural fence line, which provided complete privacy.

It was a Saturday in the late afternoon. It was late spring, so the weather was still cloudy, but not cold or rainy. It was actually one of the nicer days and all we wanted to do was be outside. We had spent pretty much all day outside and her parents told us we had about an hour before we needed to come in to help with dinner, which we did for almost every meal when we stayed the night.

For that last hour we had, we decided to play hide and seek in the part of the forest closest to the house. There were big, beautiful trees throughout — some we could hide behind, some we could climb. We did rock, paper, scissors to determine who was "it" and would be counting. The friend that had to count first picked where home base was and she picked the wishing well that was in the front yard by the house. We could hide anywhere in the trees closest to the house and we couldn't go past the orange cone that marked the halfway point in the driveway from the street to the house and we had to always be able to see the house.

So our friend started counting to fifty and the rest of us scattered and started running for the trees. My other two friends ran to the trees on the right side of the driveway and I ran to the left side. We'd been in these trees so much over the years and I always thought the left side had the best trees for hide and seek. I ran into the tree line about 10-15 feet in from the greenspace. Within about a minute, everything around me started to get dark. I looked up to the canopy of the trees to see if the sky was getting dark because I remember thinking that it wasn't that dark when we started the game a few minutes ago. So I went to a tree about ten feet deeper into the forest and hid behind it. Since it was early spring, most of the trees had leaves or were at least starting to get their leaves, which made hide and seek even better this time of year. It wasn't the biggest tree, so it wouldn't make it obvious as to where I was hiding. But there was something about this tree that felt kind of like a magnet, like I was supposed to be there.

I hid so well and was so quiet, I was really proud of myself. I didn't hear anyone or anything. Everything around me was so still and so quiet, like everything was frozen or on pause. Then I heard a whisper.

"*Hello.*"

I carefully looked around to make sure it wasn't one of my friends trying to trick me into giving away my hiding spot. There was no one and nothing. Only forest and trees. And I heard the whisper again.

"*Stay near me. Be quiet. Don't move.*"

I held my breath and stayed absolutely still. I don't know how long I didn't move and tried to breathe as shallow and as softly as I could. It felt like forever. I didn't even know who or what I was talking to, but I whispered as quietly as I could.

"Can I move now?"

"*Don't move.*" the voice quickly whispered back.

I was huddled up as close and as tight as I could to the tree and didn't move. I put my cheek on the bark of the tree so I could put my head down and breathe into the bend in my elbow and just waited to hear the whisper again.

A few minutes later, I heard it again.

"*You're safe now.*"

I asked it if I could move now.

It replied, "*Yes*".

I peeled myself off the tree and looked around. There was still no one and nothing. I looked at where I had been up against the tree. The color of its bark was slightly different in what looked like an outline of my body. I put my hand on the tree and felt the same magnet pull that I had before.

I whispered "Thank you" to the tree and walked back towards the greenspace clearing.

As I was about 5 feet from the clearing, the sky was brighter and not dark and stormy at all. I heard all my friends and my friend's parents yelling my name over and over again. I walked through the trees and they all ran to me. They told me I was gone for so long — over an hour — and they couldn't find me. They told me there were two adult coyotes that had come down the hill and were walking around the yard. My friend's parents thought they had recently come out of hibernation and were looking for small animals or food left out for outdoor pets. But we could've easily been in danger with us hiding in the forest.

Everyone asked me what happened and where I was. I had an instant realization that the tree protected me from the coyotes. It kept me safe and out of danger. But there was no way anyone was going to believe me if I told them everything that had happened in the last hour and that the tree had whispered to me to keep me safe. I just told them that I must have gone too far for me to hear them without realizing where I was. And that I was just hiding behind a tree the whole time. I never saw the coyotes. I never heard anyone calling my name. I only heard the voice whispering to me, but didn't tell them that.

Chapter Nine: The Candlelight Tour

When I was 10 years old, we moved out of Portland and to a city nearby. This city has an old military fort that is part of the area's rich history. The fort has daily tours and I'm pretty sure there has been a field trip to the fort for every elementary school student within twenty miles.

Every year in mid-autumn, the fort does a series of candlelight tours. The weather is still mild, not a lot of rain yet and not too cold at that time of year. For the candlelight tour, historical society volunteers dress up in period outfits, they have tables set with time specific pieces for dinners and the schoolhouse, they have people working in the blacksmith shop and the trade/mercantile store, they have period military weapons on display and basically make the fort come to life, as if it was fully operating during that time in history. The volunteers that dress in period clothing are like actors, where they cannot break character or their role within the community, and are extremely educated on the history of the fort, the time period and what life was like for those living in the fort.

Throughout the property, there are several buildings: a blacksmith shop, the fur traders outpost, the infirmary, mercantile store, along with some military officer's residences and barracks. There is zero electricity used during the candlelight tour. When you come and buy your ticket, you are put with a group and then led by a tour guide who is also dressed in period clothing, carrying a lantern to light the way. But unlike the volunteers throughout the tour, the tour guides are not actors and are not in character. All throughout the buildings are lanterns and candles so that as you walk through any part of the fort, you are stepping back into that time.

When I was 13 years old, my mom and I went to our first candlelight tour at the fort. I have always liked history and learning about it. So I was excited to go. We walked through the gate, got our tickets and waited for our tour guide to come get the group we were to be a part of. Since this was a living exhibit, they encouraged us not to talk or have outside conversations that would take away from the experience. I thought that was weird, but understood. Our tour guide was female and wore a period dress with a white smock apron. We had about twelve people in our group and the first place we went on the tour was one of the houses that belonged to a military officer.

The house had two stories and a wide porch all the way around the house. When we walked up the stairs to the front door, it brought us into a foyer hallway area where we filed in one by one. The foyer hallway then opened up into a sitting room. There was a fire in the fireplace, some wing-back chairs, a sofa, a chaise and a couple of small tables.

In one of the chairs, sat an older gentleman, reading a book and smoking a pipe. I thought it was weird that he'd be smoking a pipe inside, as there was no smoking in the buildings. I whispered to my mom about the guy sitting in the chair, smoking the pipe, and why they would let him do that. She looked and leaned into me and whispered that the chair was empty. I deeply inhaled, like the information scared me and realized I could smell the pipe. My grandpa had smoked a pipe and it had a distinctive smell. The fact that I was looking right at this man, watching him smoke his pipe, but my mom couldn't see him and I could smell his pipe, freaked me out completely.

We were stopped in this room while the tour guide told us about the military officer that lived in the house and also to wait for the group before us to leave the next room. He never looked up or looked at any of us. It was like we were ghosts to him. I sat there staring at him, not blinking, thinking if I did blink, he wouldn't be there. That he would disappear into thin air. As we moved from the sitting room to the kitchen, I never took my eyes off of him. And he never disappeared.

We went upstairs to see the bedrooms, which were large, ornate and luxurious for the time. With each stop during the tour, the guide would give history about the house, along with some interaction from the actors. The tour guide interacted with every actor, but never interacted with the man I saw in the sitting room.

We left the officer's house and moved to another building, a house provided for aides, helpers and servants to the officers. Again, we entered through a foyer hallway, but we bypassed the sitting room. We walked through it to get to a large dining hall area, but it was roped off and there were no actors. Once we got to the large dining area, there was the biggest dining table I'd ever seen. It must have sat twenty people. The table was set with dishes, cups, saucers and silverware. There was no food or drink on the table, as I'm sure it would not have been edible due to the length of time of the tours over the course of the evening.

Our guide stopped to talk to the "cook" and the people in the kitchen who would have served the meals to the officers. They interacted and talked about the history of the building, the officers and the roles of the people working in that building. Then something made a loud "tink" sound. I turned my head to see what it was. There was a man, dressed in full military uniform, sitting at the head of the table furthest away from where we were standing, and he had dropped his fork on the plate in front of him. I looked at my mom, who was still focused on the tour guide and the actors. I looked at the other people in our group, who were also doing the same. I looked at the tour guide and the actors, who had not even noticed this man nor heard or acknowledged the sound of the metal meeting the dish.

Now, I started to kind of freak out again. *Am I the only one who can see him or the other man? Am I the only one who smelled the vanilla pipe tobacco? Am I the only one who heard this officer drop his fork on his plate?* I seriously questioned whether or not I could finish this tour. I looked at my mom and raised my eyebrows, hoping to prompt her into asking me what's wrong. She took the cue and asked me. I whispered to her and asked if she heard a loud "tink" sound a minute ago. She said she didn't hear anything like that. So then I asked her if she saw anyone sitting at the other end of the large table. She slowly turned her head to look and studied the area for a few seconds. Then she whispered to me that she didn't see anyone there now. I looked out of the corner of my eye, so as to not make it obvious that I was trying to validate what I saw. Even out of my peripheral vision, I could still see him sitting there. It looked like he was eating a meal and taking sips out of the water (or wine) cup, even though there was no food or drink anywhere on the table. I stood a little closer to my mom so I would be comfortable.

The tour guide finished their interaction with the actors and in order to leave the dining area, we had to walk the length of the large table and exit through the door behind it. Behind where this military officer was sitting at the end of the table. Our group starts to file past the table and no one is noticing or acknowledging this man sitting at the table. Not one single person, not even the tour guide. I held my breath as we passed by the end of the table where he sat. He didn't acknowledge us either. He just focused on what he was doing, paying no attention to us.

We moved on to the next building — the infirmary. The outside appearance of the building was actually very similar to the Officer's house and the servant's house. I'm guessing it was so it didn't attract attention, in the event of a battle or war. But inside there were less walls and bigger rooms. This is where hurt soldiers and residents would come if they needed medical attention. There were a couple of smaller rooms off the larger rooms. These were for private appointments with the doctors. I suspect similar to an exam room of medical clinics today.

We are walking through the largest of the rooms on the first floor that would have been the main hospital room and looked like it could hold about 10 hospital beds comfortably. We are listening to the tour guide explain about the infirmary, the history, the doctors and some details about when it was used when the fort was active. As we are leaving that room, we pass by one of the small private rooms. Papers can be heard shuffling, footsteps on the wood floors and glass medicine bottles "tinkling", but there was no one in there. When I looked in the room, I didn't see any papers or glass bottles physically moving and there was no one in there, but you could definitely hear them from the threshold of the room as we walked by.

We continued on through the rest of the tour. No one said anything about hearing or seeing the things I heard and saw, no one reacted to any of those things while they were happening.

I have not been on another candlelight tour since, but I have taken both of my children on field trips to the fort when they were in elementary school. Those school field trips were during the day and I did not experience anything during either of them.

Chapter Ten: The Day Uncle Died

My uncle (my mom's oldest brother) was my godfather. For many years, he was the positive male influence in my life. I loved him and I spent a lot of time at his and my aunt's house when I was a kid. When I had my first child, he and my aunt drove three hours to be at the hospital when our son was born. It was really special to have them there.

One day, about 12 years ago, I got a phone call from my mom, who was absolutely wrecked. She told me that my uncle hadn't been feeling good and my aunt was taking him to the doctor to get checked out. And then told me that, as my aunt helped him into the car to go to the doctor, he had a massive heart attack and died right there in the car, still parked in the driveway. When we got the news, we were all devastated.

When my uncle died, our son was ten years old. I did not tell him right away, as I was waiting to tell my husband first, so we could tell him together. But our son came home from school that day and told us something weird kept happening to him all day. I asked him if he was feeling okay, like was he getting sick or anything? He said that he felt fine, except that all day, it felt like someone was touching his hair and his head. He described it as "You know how uncle pats me on top of my head when he sees me? That's what it feels like." I just about lost it. There was no way I couldn't *not* tell him in that moment.

So I explained as best as I could that uncle had passed away, in an age appropriate way. He asked me if I thought uncle was trying to tell him goodbye with the pats on his head that he'd been feeling all day. (This kid! He was so in tune with his gifts when he was younger, but also so just accepting of something like this.) I told him that I really thought that maybe he was. He asked if he should ask Uncle if it was him. I told him it couldn't hurt to ask him and see if he got an answer if it really was him. And then he audibly asks out loud, "Uncle, if that's you trying to say goodbye, can you push down my hair?" I waited. He waited. Then ever so slightly, I saw part of his hair flatten. At the same time I saw this (and hoping I'm not just imagining it), my son said that the top of his head tingled and felt like cobwebs, like when your hand or foot falls asleep. I was astounded at what happened. Not for me, because I've had plenty of experiences, but for my son. Like what happened and how he reacted was just so natural for him. Not scared or freaked out or anything. It was as if it had happened before and was a normal occurrence for him.

After that moment with Uncle saying goodbye to my son, he didn't feel the pats on his head, the tingling feeling or the cobwebs on his head again. That one act, that one moment gave him closure about his great-uncle passing away. I think that was more comforting to him than anything.

Chapter Eleven: The Three Angels

People say that some supernatural gifts can be hereditary. They can be the exact same gifts or something similar. I had my suspicions with our son, that he was able to see and sense spirits, similar to mine, but there had only been a few small things to make me think that. But also, children in general are just more receptive to the supernatural.

When our daughter was born, it was an amazing moment. There is 9 ½ years between our son and our daughter. It was not planned that way, but that's just how God blessed us.

When she was a little over a year old, she and I were in her bedroom one afternoon. I had her on the changing table, getting ready to change her diaper, so her point of view was the ceiling and the upper part of the walls she was facing towards.

As she laid there, she pointed up to the corner where the wall met the ceiling above her bedroom door and said, "Babies". I look to where she pointed and there were 3 white balls of light, hovering in the corner. I just couldn't stop staring at them, for fear if I blinked or moved, they would be gone.

I kept my hand on her to keep her from moving too much on the changing table, but I was just so mesmerized by what I saw. Each ball of light was maybe about three inches in diameter each. Just glowing. Just floating together in an irregular triangle pattern. My daughter kept pointing and said "Babies" two more times before they slowly faded away. When they were gone, I burst into tears. Not because the orbs scared me, but because of the significance of them.

My daughter was barely a year old when this happened and there was absolutely no way she would have understood, even if we had told her. But somehow, she knew.

The reason our children are 9 ½ years apart is partly because of some health issues my husband started having when our son was two years old and continued until he was just over five years old. However, it is mostly because in the almost three years before I got pregnant with our daughter that I had three very brutal miscarriages. I almost died from the last two. Our daughter is a rainbow baby. (If you are unfamiliar with the term "rainbow baby", a rainbow baby is a child born after a miscarriage or stillborn or a child that passed away shortly after birth.)

And there my daughter was, pointing at these three balls of light, telling me that those were "Babies". She knew what they were and was somehow connected to them. It was a moment full of awe and simultaneous heartbreak.

Chapter Twelve: Halloween Stranger

In the Pacific Northwest, it's no secret that it rains a lot. No fall, winter or spring holiday is safe from the rain, especially Halloween. It is always a 50-50 shot that we will get rain for the kids to go trick or treating.

For all the years that our kids dressed up for Halloween, we had a tradition - we would visit all the grandparents first and then go trick or treating in the neighborhood of one of our relatives.

This particular Halloween, we did that. And when we were done, we decided at the last minute that we would stop by one of our cousin's houses on the way home that lived close by. It was pouring down rain. Like it was almost impossible to actually go trick or treating because it was so wet & cold.

The distance between the houses was not far and as we turned onto the main road to get to our cousin's street, I gasped so loud, my husband stomped on the brakes. He actually got irritated with me because he thought something was wrong but couldn't see that there was something wrong.

I looked around and asked him where the man went. He looked at me like I had three heads with worms crawling out of each one.

He asked me, "What man?"

I asked him if he saw that man trying to cross the busy road. He said there was no man. I was insistent and told him that yes, there was a man. I described him in great detail — he had a black leather jacket, with blue jeans, black motorcycle boots with a silver buckle, dark brown hair and looked to be middle aged around mid-fifties. He was soaked from the rain and was just standing there, like he was trying to cross the street or was waiting to be picked up. No one saw him but me. I looked back at the direction where I saw him and he was standing there in the pouring down rain with his hands in his jacket pockets, head hanging down. No one still saw him.

We continued on to our cousin's house, only spending a little time there before heading back home. It was maybe 15-20 minutes that we were there. But to go home, we had to drive by the same spot where I saw this man. When we passed by that same spot, he was not there. I don't know if what I saw was a real person or a spirit. It certainly was enough to make me question that he was living.

Chapter Thirteen: The Closet Visitor

The house that we live in currently is a typical, standard 1960's ranch style house. In the hallway that leads to the bedrooms, we have a closet that we use for small storage and also houses our hot water heater. Inside this closet door, is also a full length mirror because it was the only place that made sense to put it, where we could all use it.

From the time our daughter was about 3 until just before she turned 7, she loved opening the closet door and looking at herself in the mirror. It was the only mirror in the house she could see herself in without having to be lifted up. We'd hear her talking to herself in the mirror and we'd always try to hear what she was saying, but she'd be whispering, mumbling or we couldn't understand what she was saying. She would spend as much as 15-20 minutes in front of the mirror at a time. It was usually once a day, but sometimes it was twice a day.

When she was about 5 years old, we finally asked her what she was saying in the mirror. She told us she was talking to the little boy in the mirror. We asked her what kinds of things she was talking about with the little boy, because mirrors can be dangerous and used as portals or tools to enchant or possess people. She told us they talked about what toys they liked to play with, what they liked to eat, about their family and things like that. Although I thought it was a little odd, I allowed it to continue, but only while one of us could be monitoring the interaction. Up to that point, it was pretty harmless stuff and nothing that would cause any red flags or concern.

One day, shortly before our daughter turned 7, she was talking to the little boy in the mirror. She talked to the mirror for about 10 minutes and then closed the door. She had a very confused look on her face. I asked her what was wrong and why she had that look on her face. She explained that the boy in the mirror said something really weird and that she didn't understand it. So I asked her what the boy had said to her. She said that he told her he was about nine years old and lived in our house for only about three months and had to move to another house quickly. She said he told her that he knew her mom and she wanted to know if I knew him. I told her that I had never talked to the boy in the mirror before and I didn't even know his name. She told me that his name was Carter.

My jaw dropped wide open and I just about fell on the floor after hearing her tell me all these things. Like complete and total shock. The age she said he was, that he knew me and what his name was.

About 3 years before I was pregnant with our daughter, I had 3 very brutal miscarriages, where I almost died from the last 2. I couldn't carry any of those pregnancies past the 1st trimester. My husband and I had already decided if the baby was a boy, we would name him Carter

James. Based on the age he said he was and the things we knew, it lines up with my first miscarriage.

I asked her if she wanted to keep talking to the boy in the mirror and she said no. So I told her that she needed to tell him that. I gave her some suggestions on what to say to him, to let him know that she couldn't talk to him anymore. She sat down on the couch and looked like she was mulling things over, trying to decide what she wanted to say. After about half an hour, she got up and opened the closet door. I sat in the living room, waiting to hear what she was going to say. She was more or less whispering and it kind of sounded like she was talking to herself. But I could just barely make out part of what she was telling him. Something about how she was sorry, but she didn't feel good talking to him anymore and she didn't want him to be lonely, but that she wanted him to find good friends and had to say goodbye. It was very heartfelt and sincere, but also very mature. I was very proud of her. From that moment on, she did not talk to the boy in the mirror anymore. She never mentioned it or him and it was almost like — in her mind — that it was so long ago, she couldn't even really remember him.

We hadn't talked about or even thought about the little boy in the mirror for about a year. Until one morning, it crept up on me — literally.

Our current house is pretty dark inside at night, with only a small amount of light that gets past the front curtains from the street light outside at the corner of our front property. It's just enough light to distinguish where furniture is, with different shades of dark. Our hardwood floors are medium-light colored, so any piece of furniture or form can be seen without too much trouble.

This particular morning, I had to get up early and it was before the sun was up. I don't remember what I had to do that day that warranted an extra early morning, but my husband was already gone for work, as he often is at that time of morning.

Our bedroom is at the end of the hall and the closet is at the beginning of the hallway, with the bathroom in between. So I opened the bedroom door to go to the bathroom and when I left the bedroom, I had to look up the hallway to get to the bathroom.

As I stepped into the hallway and closed the bedroom door, I saw a small figure of a boy, crouched down against the wall directly next to the closet. He sat on the floor with his back up against the wall, knees pulled to his chest and his arms wrapped around his knees, chin tucked and resting his forehead on his knees. It took me by surprise and I just stood there looking at him. I could feel the sadness he felt. I could feel the loneliness he felt.

I spoke to him and told him I could see him. He lifted his head from his knees just enough to nod at me that he acknowledged me acknowledging him. I asked him if he was the little boy in the mirror that had been talking to my daughter. He lifted his head again and barely nodded. Then I asked if he was in fact Carter. He lifted his head and looked at me.

"Yes. You know me, Mama."

Tears streamed down my face. What I had suspected was true. I asked him why he was here. He told me he was lonely and that by talking to our daughter, he got to see a small part of what would have been his life, his family.

By this time, I was sobbing, a complete hot mess of tears, snot and emotions, still staring at him as best as I can through the tears, trying to find my voice. I finally managed to get my brain working again and tell him how much we had already loved him, how devastated we were when he couldn't be here with us and how much we missed him. I explained that he wouldn't be lonely if he could find his way back home to God, to the light, and encouraged him to go back home so he could be loved how he needed to be loved.

He lifted his head, thanked me for giving him the words that I spoke to him and started to stand. He got up, turned towards the closet and just faded away into nothing. After that interaction, we never saw him or heard him again.

I have never had an encounter like that before and have yet to have one like that since. I think that him talking to our daughter through the mirror and him appearing that morning was a manifestation of some emotions that I perhaps hadn't fully dealt with but were lingering. But I also think it was the healing and closure he needed, and I needed, so that neither of us were hurting anymore.

Chapter Fourteen: And the Band Played On

For as long as my husband and I have been together, he has listened to music at night (most nights) when trying to fall asleep. He doesn't listen to it every single night, but I would say he does about 60% - 70% of the time. Thank God for headphones and AirPods! Before iPods, Bluetooth headphones, earbuds, and AirPods, he had a small stereo boombox on his side of the bed, where he would listen to music or sometimes his favorite talk show — *Love Line*. You know? The one with Dr. Drew and Adam Carolla? If you are an 80's-90's kid, you have to know about *Love Line*. Anytime it was on, he would listen to it. I believe it was once a week for a significant block of time, like 3 or 4 hours.

But Thank God, for headphones! Because I didn't have to listen to what he was listening to anymore. It's not that I didn't enjoy it, but there were times when I wanted to watch TV or have no sound at all, even over the fan we run all year long for white noise. I didn't have to ask him to turn down the volume or once he was asleep, get up and turn it off for him.

Over the many, many years of our relationship, I have lost track of the number of times I've asked him to turn down his music, only to be told that he wasn't playing any. I have heard loud music playing when there wasn't any sound to be heard by him. All types of music ranging from classical to soft rock, to pop to country. It was all loud, plain as day, so much that I could hum the tune or sing along with the words. This wasn't some "ear worm" where a song got stuck in my head. The songs would change when each one was over, like a radio station or a playlist. And every time I would ask him to turn the music down, either it was too loud over the speakers or I could hear it coming through his headphones, he would look at me like I had worms crawling out of my eye sockets.

There have been times, more than I can count, when I asked him to turn down his music and he told me he wasn't listening to music. And that he was listening to *Love Line* or a podcast with no music, only people talking. There have been other times, more than I can count, that I've asked him to turn down the music, only for him to tell me he wasn't listening to anything at all.

This same type of experience has happened at other times too, in other situations. I will have just gotten home and pulled into the driveway or just parked my car somewhere and there is that 10-20 seconds of silence from when I turn off the car, get my phone and my purse and then get out. And as soon as I've turned off the car, I can hear a full band or a full symphony or a full song with heavy bass. Only when I open the car door, is it complete silence.

Chapter Fifteen: My Talk With Jesus

Back early in mine and my husband's relationship, we went through a rough patch. We had been together for 2 years, were out on our own for the first time, we were new parents at 20 and 21 years old, both working full-time jobs and trying to make ends meet. Everything seemed to irritate us. Everything was super stressful. Everything seemed to be an uphill battle. We never fought before and it seemed like that's all we did when we were home together. It was not a good time in our relationship at all.

It came to the point where I couldn't take it anymore. I asked him to go to counseling and he refused. I had already made up my mind before I asked him that if he didn't go to counseling, I would give him an ultimatum: go to counseling together or we needed to live separately for a little while. So I did one of the hardest things I had ever done in my life up to that point and asked him to leave. Because I loved him and I didn't want to hate him. Because we both needed to work on things individually and together to have any chance of a successful relationship going forward.

For over a year, we didn't live together. I still lived in our apartment with our son and my best friend moved in to help me cover rent. He lived with his grandparents about 10 minutes away. We did all the things we thought we should do. He paid me child support every time he got paid. He came up to the apartment to spend time with our son. I took our son down to his grandparents' house to spend time with him. We talked consistently and eventually learned how to communicate properly. It hurt my heart that it had to be this way, but I knew it was the only way for both of us to be healthy, individually and together.

After the fresh hurt wore off, I realized the separation was necessary. But I prayed everyday that we would be a family again. I prayed that he would be the husband and father I knew he could be. I prayed that I could be the wife and mother he and our son needed. I practically begged God to make us a family again.

It had been about 10 months since we had not lived together. I had just gotten back to the apartment with our son from visiting him. I put our son to bed and went to my bedroom, shut the door and just started sobbing uncontrollably. I wanted him to come home, but I wasn't sure if he was ready. I cried out to Jesus, "Please, just make us a family again." And I cried and cried.

I was laying in my bed curled up, sobbing, when someone said my name. The only other person at the apartment was our son and he was not old enough to talk. Even if he could, he would not call me by my name.

I held my breath so as not to make a single noise, trying to figure out if I had imagined it. And also so I didn't freak out, thinking I had completely lost it. In complete silence, I heard someone say my name again. It was a male voice, very soft, very gentle. I thought to myself, *Should I answer?* So, very quietly, and with as much courage as I could muster in that moment, I said, "Yes?" And I raised my head and looked around. There was no one standing in my room. I was not expected to hear anything else and I had heard of people under extreme duress having hallucinations.

But the voice spoke again. It said, "You WILL be a family again. Do not worry any longer. Your relationship is blessed and protected."

I asked the voice "Are you sure?"

And it answered "Yes. It is what you've been praying for." And I just sat there in awe, in amazement, in shock.

I had never told anyone what I wanted or what I had prayed for. And the voice said back to me exactly what I had been praying for. In that moment of immense pain and heartache, that moment of revelation, I know without a shadow of a doubt that I had a supernatural interaction with Jesus. There is no other explanation and no other possibility.

It was a profound experience that I will never forget. 4 months later, we moved into another apartment, together, and we were a family again. That entire 2 minute interaction increased my faith exponentially and completely changed the trajectory of our relationship into something not even could be done justice in the movies. I am forever grateful for that experience.

Extra Content: The Curious Case of Mr. Black

★ *Note — the names of the people involved in this experience have been changed to keep and maintain anonymity.*

I knew Kenny Black through a previous employer of mine. Kenny was business partners with my boss, Derek. Derek had his own technology business, whom I worked for. But they had another business that they were partners in, where Kenny ran it and Derek was more of a silent partner.

I came to know Kenny, as he was in our office once a month for him and Derek to sign checks. I also did some specific tasks for Kenny's business and learned a lot about it. And as I worked for Derek, Kenny and his wife, Michelle, often attended many of our company events. I got to know Michelle well. We actually both ended up pregnant at the same time and our daughters are less than a month apart in age.

I had worked for Derek for about five years when he and Kenny decided to part ways and no longer be business partners. Kenny bought Derek out of his part of the business and I trained Michelle on how to do the tasks I had been doing for Kenny's company.

I worked for Derek for almost seven years, until it was no longer a good place to work. And because I knew the specifics of Kenny's business well, he sought me out to come work for him and I accepted. In just over six months after starting, I became Kenny's right hand. I helped him with everything — worked deals with him, helped him with clients and vendors, he would brainstorm growth ideas with me, I would fill in for him when he was out of town or on vacation. Everyone in our industry, all of our vendors and all of our clients saw me as second in command. We all worked from home and we always were productive and growing the company. It wasn't really his style to sit and look over your shoulder constantly.

In December of 2016, Kenny suffered a major medical event. While there wasn't any physical impairment or long term effects stemming from the major medical event, we all soon realized there were changes in some of his mental cognitive abilities. He would easily forget things and he had difficulty finding correct words for things. He would pause or trip over words to find the one he was looking for. His spelling and grammar had always been questionable in emails and written correspondence, but now it was atrocious. Like if you didn't know him, you would think he only had an elementary school education, not a college education. Too many times to count from 2016 on, I would have partners, clients or vendors reach out to me to interpret Kenny's emails and voicemails because the words were jumbled and couldn't make sense of what he was trying to say, the question he was trying to ask or the point he was trying to get across.

But in July of 2018, Kenny really changed. Everything about him became different and frustrating. He would anger easily, he started to micro-manage everyone, including partners, vendors and clients. He was irritable and easily angered, as if he literally had zero patience with anyone and everyone. When you talked to him, you never knew which Kenny you were going to get - the old Kenny, who was caring, understanding and nice to be around or the new Kenny, who was volatile, unpredictable, rude and sometimes even mean. He was very difficult to talk to, work with or be around. His behavior didn't go unnoticed by others who worked for him, as well as some vendors and a few clients. It came down to them working with anyone else but him. He burned a lot of bridges and ended a lot of long-term friendships over his change in behavior and mood.

The stress was too much for me, and in December 2018, I told Kenny I was going to resign at the end of the month, but would stay on as a contractor to continue doing the bookkeeping for him. Michelle kept the bookkeeping software on her computer at their house, so I'd still get to see both of them at least once a month, which was important to me because of the deep friendship Michelle and I had.

I had already been offered a position at another company and could start as soon as I wanted to. Two of our other main staff members also told him they would be resigning at the end of the month. In a matter of days, he found out he was losing me and two of our key employees. He was devastated. He was mad, angry, sad, depressed and had a whole array of in-between emotions for the duration that I worked for him. I had never seen or heard him cry before in all the time I knew him. But in the days leading up to my last day, he was so overwhelmed with everything, he sobbed to me one day on the phone about everyone leaving him.

I only saw him two more times after my last day working for him, both of which were up at his and Michelle's house when I came to do the monthly bookkeeping visit. Two months after I left his company, on a Friday, I got a text from Michelle:

Kenny's dead. I'm so overwhelmed.

I read the text about a dozen times, trying to figure out the tone of it. Did he do something as a joke and now she's pissed? Or was this a crossroads in their marriage? Or did he in fact, die? So after a few minutes, I finally managed to text her back, trying to gauge the situation.

What?!?! What happened??

Her next text was short, but tells me everything.

Allison and I are next door at the neighbor's house. The police and the coroner is at the house. I will call you in a little while.

Holy crap! Oh my God! He really is dead. It wasn't a joke or anything like that. I wanted to go hug my friend. I wanted to know what happened to Kenny and how I could help her.

I was antsy as I waited for her call. I don't know if "little while" is 15 minutes or 2 hours. I paced around my house, trying to find anything that would occupy me so I don't drive myself crazy. Finally, after about 90 minutes, she called me, upset and overwhelmed. She almost sounded like she was in the middle of a panic attack. I asked her how she was and what I could do to help her and Allison. She said she was numb and so overwhelmed that her brain didn't work at the moment, but as she came out of the fog, maybe she'd have an answer for me.

I asked her if she was able to tell me what happened. She explained that Kenny wasn't feeling good that morning. He was just exhausted and thought maybe he was starting to get a cold. He was just sitting in his chair in the living room watching TV for most of the morning. Then he went downstairs to his office to check email and his appointments. She said he wouldn't stay down there for very long, maybe just a few minutes, and then come back upstairs to his chair. She said she had to leave for a couple of appointments and reminded him that he was supposed to pick up Allison from school. He said he remembered and that it was on his calendar. He told her he was going to take it easy because he just was not feeling good.

Michelle said that earlier that day, in the afternoon, she had two missed calls from Allison's school. So she called the school, where they told her that Allison was still at school and Kenny hadn't come to pick her up. Michelle asked the school if they'd tried to get a hold of Kenny and they said they'd tried twice on his cell phone and twice on his office phone. She hung up with the school and tried to call Kenny on his cell phone. She left a voicemail and then sent a text. She then called his office phone, trying to drive to get to the school as quickly as she could, so it was difficult for her to keep calling and texting. She prayed that he called or texted her back while on her way to the school. But he didn't.

She got to the school and picked up Allison. About 10 minutes later, they got to their house and Kenny's truck was still in the driveway. Michelle told Allison to stay in the car because something was not right. Michelle called the next door neighbor and asked if she could come get Allison from the car and take her to her house because something wasn't right and if it isn't, like her gut is telling her it's not, she doesn't want her to see it or be involved.

The neighbor walked down to get Allison, while Michelle waited for them to start back to the neighbor's house, unsure of what she's going to find after unlocking the front door. When she opened the door, she yelled for him. No answer. But she heard something else.

Water running from somewhere. She turned her head to get a better listen as to where the water is coming from, thinking she heard where it is running and walked down the hall to the bathroom. The door was closed, but she could hear the shower running. Michelle knocked on the door and yelled his name. No answer. She knocks and yells his name again. Still no answer. She opened the bathroom door and immediately screamed, finding Kenny hunched over the side of the bathtub, head under the running water. She thought he maybe slipped trying to fix the shower for himself. But there was no doubt that he was dead.

She frantically called 911 and the police came out to investigate. The police called the coroner and they also came out while the police were there. What the coroner suspected happened was that Kenny had a major heart attack — a myocardial infarction, otherwise known as the "Windowmaker heart attack". She explained that the coroner said most people who die from this complain they aren't feeling good the day or two leading up to the heart attack, they experience some uncontrollable stomach and/or bowel issues and the coroner speculated that maybe Kenny was going to take a shower to either feel better or clean up, as there was feces all over the toilet, the floor and the wall near the toilet.

Michelle told me that finding him in bed with another woman would have been easier to process and less devastating than finding Kenny like that. She said that she and Allison were going to stay the night at the neighbors' house until the police were finished at the house, as well as getting the house cleaned. While the police were still there, she managed to get some pajamas and clothes for both of them, so she didn't have to be in the house by herself. And all she wanted to do was have something to eat, a glass of wine and a hot bath.

I was speechless. I couldn't believe what happened. I didn't say much, just acknowledgement that I was listening. I just let her talk as much as she wanted. Because I think allowed it to help her process everything that had happened that day. I think it was cathartic for her to get the words out. Saying the words out loud may have been the only thing she could control at that moment.

When she finished talking, we agreed that we would talk on Monday, while the house got cleaned and she could figure out what she needs to do next. I told her that I loved her and to let me know what I could do to help.

Over the weekend, I texted her a couple of times, checking in with her and to see how she and Allison were doing. She said Allison was extremely sad and upset about losing her dad and that she, herself, was just trying to figure out what to do first and when she can make herself go back in the house. Then she asked me if I could come up to the house with her on Monday because there was a deadline that needed to be met for Kenny's business and hoped I could help with that, as well as help get his emails caught up. I told her that, of course, I would come help her with anything she needed.

I had been to their house hundreds of times. The drive up there was no different than every time before. But everything about this time was so different. When I got to the house, Michelle was waiting outside for me. I think it was as much of a preparation for her as it was for me. She told me she had forced herself to go in the house the day before and again before I got there. I could tell she was still shaken up, nervous, completely freaked out.

Their house was built on a hill, where facing the front of the house, it just looked like a single-story. But there was an entire full basement that you can only see from the back side of the house, with a wrap-around porch above it from the main level.

The front door was just to the left of the garage. When you walked into the house through the front door, you could either go right and head downstairs to the basement or you could go forward and it would take you to the rest of the main level of the house. By walking straight from the front door, there was a hallway on the left, which took you to a bedroom, a bathroom and the master suite.

When I walked in the house that day, it was like there was a black curtain hanging over the entrance to that side hallway on the main level. If you continued straight past that hallway, it would take you to the main living room and the kitchen. But every time I walked past that hallway, it didn't register in my brain that there was actually a hallway there. It was like there was a barrier or wall there that no one was supposed to cross.

A lot of my time spent at their house had always been in Michelle's office, Kenny's office or the kitchen. So when I arrived, just like every other time, Michelle had coffee waiting for me. We each fixed ourselves a cup and headed downstairs to Kenny's desk. Since I had been Kenny's right hand gal for so many years, it was the easiest for me to step in to figure out where he had left off with completing this project by the deadline, as well as catching up on his emails.

I sat down in his chair, at his desk, in front of his computer. Once I got everything open that I needed to do the project, I let Michelle know that I've got this handled and she can go do whatever she needs to do. While we were getting our coffee, she had listed a bunch of stuff that she had to do with getting the death certificate, life insurance, funeral arrangements and a bunch of other things. So I didn't want her to worry about trying to get this done on top of everything else.

She walked down the hallway to her office and gets settled into doing what she needs to do, so I dive right in to get this project done. I'd been sitting at Kenny's desk for about thirty minutes and I could feel something very upset and angry behind me. I turned around and saw nothing, but I could still feel the energy from it.

About twenty minutes later, I heard shuffling noises coming from this spare bedroom next to where Kenny's desk was. I wouldn't exactly call it a bedroom, because there's no way you could fit an adult sized bed or even a kid sized bed in there. It was more of a large, oversized closet. And that's exactly what Kenny used it for — his closet. It sounded like someone was rifling through the dresser drawers and looking through all the items hung on the hangers. It was actually quite loud. So loud that I said Michelle's name, thinking it was her, and there was no answer.

I got up and peeked around the corner into the closet to find it empty of any person — living or dead. I went to sit back down at Kenny's desk and had to fight through this angry energy to get back to the chair. It was like being caught in a windstorm, walking through quicksand. It was incredibly weird and I've never felt something like that before.

When I finally managed to get to the chair and sit down, it dawned on me that this could be Kenny and that he could be angry at me for sitting in his chair, at his desk, in front of his computer. I can't remember a time where he let anyone voluntarily be in that position.

I heard Michelle on the phone down the hallway, so I audibly asked if that was him. I get a very deep thrumming. It wasn't a growl and it wasn't a verbal response. But it was an unnatural noise that was a mixture of both. So I straight up ask him if he's mad at me for sitting in his chair at his desk and doing his work. All I heard was an angry, "*YES!*"

I wish I had a digital recorder running at that very moment because no one would've believed it if they'd heard it otherwise. It shocked me at first, with a big adrenaline surge. Once I realized it was him, I calmly told him, "I've got to finish this and I'm sorry I'm in your space." And I kept on working. The angry, upset energy was still there, like he was looking over my shoulder to see what I was doing and making sure I was doing it correctly. But the magnitude of the energy was less.

I wasn't sure how Michelle would perceive this information, considering her husband has been dead for just about 72 hours. But also I wasn't sure what her level of belief was around the paranormal and supernatural. It wasn't a topic that we ever talked about. So until I figured that out, I was going to keep this experience to myself.

I went up to the house everyday that week to complete this project. On one of those days the following week, Kenny was still doing normal things, for him at least. While I was downstairs in Kenny's office, at his desk, I could hear someone walking around upstairs in the kitchen and in the living room. Kenny's office was right under the kitchen, so it was very obvious the noises I was hearing. I would have totally discounted the normal sounds, except for the fact that I was at the house by myself. And later on, I will find out that this was not the first time he'd been heard in the kitchen and living room in the past week or so.

It was clear as day and as real as a physical human. I heard him walking back and forth in the kitchen, just as he would have if he was making food and going back and forth between the cupboards, the stove and the fridge. Then I heard him walk to the living room, sit down in his leather chair (and if you've ever had leather furniture of any kind, you know it makes a very distinctive sound), and turn on the TV. Kenny would often do this in between projects around the house and property and also for breaks from work.

I sat there for a few minutes, listening for any more noises and movement. I could hear the TV and I could hear Kenny shifting in the leather chair every so often. I finally convinced myself to go upstairs and actually see what was going on. And also reason with myself on what I would do if I actually see Kenny sitting in his leather chair.

I got up out of Kenny's chair at his desk and quietly walked up the stairs. I honestly didn't know if me being quiet or not would have any effect on what I would or would not see when I got upstairs, but also I wanted to be able to keep listening for the sounds I was hearing. I crept up the stairs as stealthily as I could, almost crawling. I got to the top of the stairs and rounded into the main hallway that led from the front door to the upper level of the house. Just before I reached the end of the hallway that would take me to the living room, I took a deep breath and held it, pausing to hear the same things I heard when I was downstairs.

I could hear the TV. I could hear Kenny shift or move in the leather chair. My heart raced, partly because I was still holding my breath, but mostly because I had no idea what or who I would see in the living room. I took three slow steps towards the living room, exhaled, and took two more before I was in the doorway of the living room. The TV was on the Netflix home screen, which Kenny watched quite often. The TV was not on earlier because no one was watching TV, no one else was currently home and they had no pets who could accidentally push buttons on the remote. But no one was visibly sitting in the leather chair. Even though I fully expected to see Kenny occupying his favorite chair, there was no physical person or apparition that I saw with my naked eye.

But I was still hearing the shifting of the leather on the chair, which was probably the oddest thing for my brain to register. I heard it happen, but there was nothing there to make that noise. I stared at the chair, not blinking, trying to see if I was missing something or if I could catch something. I heard it again.

So I got brave.

I called out, "Hey Kenny. I didn't know you were up here. I'm going to head back down to finish working. You good?"

And I waited to see if I could hear an answer. I didn't hear any verbal response. So I left the living room and started heading back down the hallway to the stairs. I was about two steps out of the living room and a step down the hall and the TV turned off. I stopped hearing the leather as he shifted in the chair. I froze in place, not knowing what was going on or what was going to happen next. Suddenly the temperature dropped around me quite significantly, to where the hardwood floor felt frozen underneath my feet and I was chilled to the bone. The cold lasted about twenty seconds and then just as quickly as it came, the temperature rose back up. I stood there, shocked, just waiting to hear any sounds or see anything. There was nothing but me and complete silence.

At that moment, I made a decision that the next time I was at the house, I would bring my digital recorder. And if I got the opportunity to do an EVP session, I would. So when I got home later that afternoon, I stuck my digital recorder in my purse.

I was back up at the house two days after that to continue working at Kenny's desk. But he was trying to make that difficult for me that day. Downstairs in Kenny's office area was a bank of light switches that controlled the lights for his office area, the bonus/playroom and the hallway down to Michelle's office. I came downstairs and flipped the switch to turn on the lights in Kenny's office area, but nothing happened. Instead, it turned on the light in the bonus room. I flipped that switch off and flipped on the switch for the bonus room, thinking maybe I accidentally flipped the wrong one the first time. The light in the bonus room turned on. Like I am 100% positive I flipped the right one when I first came downstairs. I know for a fact there is no way that both switches control the same set of lights. So I flip the bonus room lights off and flip the switch I know is for the hallway. The hallway lights come on.

Okay. So now I'm confused. I flipped on the switch for the lights in Kenny's office area again. This time no lights came on at all. Not in the bonus room, not in the hallway and not in the office area. Now I was frustrated because I knew I was flipping the right switches. There were three switches for three different sets of lights in three separate areas. It's not hard. I spent the next minute or two flipping all the switches individually and at the same time. Not one time did the office light come on. And the switches turned different things on. The same switch didn't turn on the bonus room lights two times in a row. And the same switch didn't turn on the hallway lights two times in a row. And no matter which switch I flipped, the office light would not turn on.

Now I was just pissed. I just spent probably about five minutes total trying to get the light on so I could get working on stuff. At this point, the game Kenny was trying to play annoyed me, and I called him out on it.

I said, "Hey, Kenny! Knock it off! I just want to get to working on stuff and get it done quickly. I need you to stop messing with the lights. So fix the lights now, please."

I stood there, waiting to see if there was some sort of response. I only had to wait about ten seconds when this static charged energy came near me. It lasted for about fifteen seconds and then slowly faded. When it was gone, I flipped the switch that I know is for the light in the office area and the light came on. I told him, "Thank you! I appreciate it," and sat down at his desk to start working.

That same day, Michelle had to run some errands and Allison had gone back to school after a month off, which left me at the house by myself. So I took the opportunity to do a couple of EVP recording sessions on my own. (EVP = electronic voice phenomenon)

(Just to note, I am not holding the recorder during any of the recordings. It is set down on a flat surface in the area near where I'm standing.)

Here are the transcripts of those 2 EVP sessions I did that day:

The responses I received are in bold *italic*. If there is nothing in bold *italic* after the question, it means I didn't get a response.

EVP Session #1:

Hi, this is Paige. And I'm at Kenny and Michelle's house. It is April 17th.

And Kenny, (deep sigh by me) I don't know what's going on, but I think you're still here.

(shuffling starts on microphone and continues for several seconds)

And if you are, come talk to me 'cause it's just weird without you and there's a lot of people who miss ya.

And so, if you just wanna come, if you're here, come talk to me in the microphone I've got in my hand, I know you know what it is.

So... and I've heard you rummaging for your clothes, I've heard you watching TV, you know we've all kind of heard ya.

So... um... just come... if you're here, come say hi into the recorder, let us know that you're here.

If you have anything to say um... let us know.

(PAUSE in me talking)

(You can hear me swallow, but there is some other sound/noise/voice in the background on the recording that I can't make out what is.)

Kenny, do you know you're dead?

Do you miss Allison?

Are you trying to get our attention by doing things like with the TV and um... the lights and the light switches?

Is there anybody else here besides Kenny? And if so, can you tell us your name?

(There is a voice, very faint, but can't make out who it is or what it says)

If you're able to, come talk to me in this microphone.

Do you know how you died?

How are you related to this property?

Can you tell us why you're here?

(There is a noise that is unclear and indistinguishable)

Is there anything that you want to say... um... to be heard? I'm here to help you be heard. You know I can see you, I can hear you, I can sense you. Um... sometimes I can't always hear you with my naked ear, but this is going to help us be able to hear you.

Kenny, does it upset you that I'm here, that I'm helping Michelle, that I'm sitting at your desk?

Yep.

Because I hope not.

Mm-hmm

I'm only here to help and make sure that Allison and Michelle are taken care of.

Mm-hmm

But I know that first day you were upset with me. You couldn't understand why I was sitting at your desk. Are you still upset with me?

Well, I hope you were able to communicate a little bit and um...for us to be able to help you and whoever else is here on this property and in this house. And um... hopefully we can talk to you again.

(There are clicking noises which is me trying to turn off the recorder.)

A little while later that same day, I did another EVP session in a different room.

EVP Session #2:

Kenny, it's Paige. Are you in here? Are you in your closet right now? I know that this space down here was your space *(Mm-hmm)* with your closet and your desk and this is where you spent a lot of time.

If you're here, can you just say your name or say yes? Um... to let me know that you're here?

Did you love this house?

Is that why you've come back? Or that you're still here... you never kind of left?

Just let me know that you're here. I just wanna know if you are or if you're not, who I'm talking to.

(Kenny's voice, but can't make out what he says)

If it's not Kenny who I'm talking to, can you tell me your name?

(There are clicking noises from me trying to turn off the recorder)

Once we got through the first couple of weeks after Kenny died, I still was up at the house a couple days a week. While we were having lunch during one of those days, Michelle told me that she had been thinking a lot about keeping the company going, with her in charge, but that she couldn't do it without me because of all my years of knowledge. She asked me if I would help her run the company. Of course, I said yes and told her that I never wanted to leave in the first place, but after Kenny's change in behavior, he made every day unbearable.

That's when she said what I'd been wanting to bring up, but didn't know how. She asked me if I thought Kenny was still in the house.

Before I could stop myself, I blurted out, "Hell yeah, I do!" Only because I was so shocked and so excited that I didn't have to have this really awkward conversation with my friend. So I managed to ask her why she asked that. She explained that she has felt him in the house with her, like he was watching her or following her.

She then explained that she had some odd experiences since Kenny's death and it was stuff that he would do when he was alive. She went on to tell me about hearing him in the living room, sitting in his leather chair. And also when she leaves the house, she always goes through the garage and always keeps the front door locked. But when Kenny would leave to go anywhere, he'd always use the front door and it would be unlocked. She said that she had found the front door unlocked at least four times since he died and was pretty sure she had heard the lock move itself once and the front door unlocked on its own. She also said that she would hear someone walking around in the kitchen, which was a place Kenny spent a lot of time, as he loved cooking and made most of the family meals.

Then she asked me why I think he's still in the house. So I start with the story about hearing him in the kitchen and then hearing him in his leather chair, watching TV and what all happened with that. Since she already shared that she had heard the same thing, I didn't want to start with something that would shock her or upset her. I wanted to be able to gauge her reaction and her receptiveness. And then I told her about the game he played with the light switches downstairs.

Then I dove into the story about what happened when I was sitting at his desk 3 days after he died, the angry energy and the noises I heard in the closet, like someone was looking for clothes. Michelle's eyes got so wide and her jaw dropped open, I wasn't sure if I had said anything wrong or said something that upset her. She asked me if she had told me exactly how Kenny had died. I told her what she had said to me about it was that he was face down in the shower, leaning over the tub with the water running. And then she tells me that he was also naked and that what I heard, rummaging in his closet for clothes, was absolutely him.

I was at a loss for words. I had no clue about him being naked when he died, which confirmed and explained my experience when I was sitting at his desk. After lunch, I asked Michelle if she would be okay with us trying to talk to him by doing an EVP session. That we could ask him some direct questions and help him to move on, so his soul could be at rest and that she would have peace again in the house. She said she would be open to that, as long as we protected ourselves. I explained that yes, I would put together a prayer and a blessing, along with some questions, as well as something to help him move on and leave the house. I told her we could do it the next time I'm up at the house in a few days. I did not tell her that I already had done 2 short EVP sessions on my own. I know she wouldn't have been mad at me about doing the EVP sessions. However, I didn't know how she would react to hearing the recordings.

I wrote out a prayer, a blessing, a list of questions and another prayer to help move Kenny on, as well as brought my digital recorder to record the interaction on that Saturday. Allison was gone at her aunt and uncle's house, so it was a perfect opportunity for Michelle and I to do this alone.

We discussed where the best place would be to do the EVP session and we agreed that down in the area where his desk and closet seemed to have a lot of energy and activity.

I set down the digital recorder on the corner of Kenny's desk and pushed the record button. When it started recording, I stated the date and location for documentation and then read the prayer that I had prepared.

This is a transcription of the recording of what I read:

"Father God,

Thank you for your gift and your blessings. Thank you for always surrounding us in your light and in your love.

"As we go forth with this EVP session, we thank you for the hedge of protection you have placed around us. We thank you that because of your protection, that no harm will come to us before, during or after this session. We are covered by the blood of Jesus.

"Thank you for being with Michelle and Allison, that you are there to comfort them, protect them and give them peace. Thank you for helping Allison to no longer be afraid to be by herself or afraid to be in this house.

"Your perfect love drives out all fear and we thank you that this house and our lives are full of only your love, your light and your peace.

"Thank you that we can communicate with Kenny to bring peace and closure. And that afterwards, you may help him and any other spirits to move on to wherever they are supposed to go.

"We pray all these things in the name of Jesus.

"Amen."

Michelle echoed the "Amen" and we gave a little pause after I finished the prayer. Then I pulled out the list of questions I had prepared so we could see if Kenny would answer us.

Before I began asking the questions, I wanted to establish why we were there and what the boundaries were.

This is a transcription of the recording of what I read:

"We are here to communicate with Kenny and any other positive spirits who might be here. This is the time to step forward, to be heard. So I've set my recorder on the edge of the table for you to communicate. Speak as loud as you can into the microphone and this will allow us to hear you clearly, when we can't hear you with our naked ears.

"Before we begin, we want to set some boundaries – before, during and after this communication session, you are not allowed to attach yourself at all to any of us. We are protected by the blood of Jesus and you are not to follow us home or anything like that.

"We also have protection tools – a rose quartz crystal, holy water- blessed by a priest and a rosary, also blessed by a priest. Any negative or malicious spirits are not welcome during this session, in this space, in any of our houses or in our lives. Is that understood?

"But Kenny and any other positive spirits, you can use our energy and the energy in this house to manifest your energy to do things to let us know you are here by talking into the recorder, making noises – like knocking on the walls, moving something. We would appreciate it if you would not touch us during this session. Do not touch us, pull our hair, touch our clothing. That is not okay. You are not invited to do that. If you want to manifest into some form of energy, like a ball of light or a mist or a shadow. If you have enough energy to do that, then please do so. We would really prefer verbal communication over physical manifestation. So we just want to talk. If you understand, please say yes into the microphone."

I pause, to allow for an answer.

Then I moved on to the questions.

And paused after I asked each question to allow for us to hear an answer when I played the recording back, to know if our questions were answered or not, to know if we connected with anything or not.

For the duration of the entire EVP session, the recorder was on the corner of Kenny's desk. The only time I touched it was to place the recorder at the beginning and at the end.

Below is the transcript of the EVP session:

(The responses I received are in bold ***italic***. If there is nothing in bold ***italic*** after the question, it means I didn't get a response.)

We have some questions that we'd like to ask Kenny directly.

Can you say your name into the microphone, so that we know it's you?

Can you do something to let us know you're here? Something audibly that we can hear, like knock on the wall, make a sound, move something?

Kenny, do you know you're dead?

No

Are you angry that you're dead?

Are you upset about all the changes like with Michelle running the company or getting rid of all your stuff?

Do you make yourself known to Allison?

Do you know that you are scaring her?

(Michelle quietly gasps after I ask this question.)

Do you mean to scare her or are you just trying to get her attention?

Are you trying to talk to Allison?

Yeah

Do you miss Allison?

(There are more questions that we asked Kenny after this, but are personal and private that I will not share the questions or the answers to, out of respect for Michelle and Allison.)

Thank you, Kenny, for your answers. We do have some other questions to ask.

How many spirits are here with us?

Can you say the number into the recorder or make a noise for the number of spirits that are here? Like knocking or tapping equal to the number of spirits?

Who else is here with us? Can you say your name?

Is there any other information you wish to share with us? Or a message that you'd like to deliver?

Thank you for manifesting all the energy that you could to come talk to us. We very much appreciate it and the answers you've given.

At the end, I read the prayer I had prepared to help move Kenny and any other spirits on, so that Michelle and Allison could reclaim peace in their house.

This is the transcription of the recording of what I read:

"Father God,

"Thank you for allowing us to communicate with Kenny and the other spirits. Thank you for the constant and vigilant protection that you surround us with. We ask that you help move those spirits to wherever they are supposed to go in the afterlife, so that they too may have peace.

"Thank you, in the name of Jesus.

"Amen."

When we were done, and everything had been asked, and everything had been said, I turned the recorder off. Michelle and I stayed down in Kenny's office for a few more minutes, while I checked in with her to see how she was doing after all that. She said it was a little overwhelming, but that she felt fine and was okay.

To this day, Michelle has never listened to the audio recording of the EVP session with both the questions and answers. But I don't really think she needed to. I do wish I had kept the recorder on for about 5 minutes longer. Because about 3 minutes after we were done with the EVP session, we both heard loud footsteps walking, almost stomping through the main hallway upstairs, to the front door. Then we both heard the front door unlock, heard the door open and aggressively slam shut. Again, Michelle and I were the only ones in the house.

We just sat there in silence, mouths open in surprise, staring at each other. I thought Michelle's eyes were going to pop out of her head. Either that or cry or scream. Finally, she started rubbing her hands over her arms, up and down trying to rid them of the almost permanent goosebumps, and finally she said "Oh. My. God. Did you hear that? Please tell me you heard that too! Do you think it was him?" I told her that I absolutely believed it was him.

Not knowing what was going to happen next, we just stood there in Kenny's office, silent and motionless, waiting. After a couple of minutes, I asked her what she felt. She said she did not feel him in the house anymore and that all she felt was silence, an empty house. I told her that I felt the same and that the energy had changed. I reminded her to just keep vigilant about what she and Allison see and hear, to make sure Kenny really had moved on.

Michelle and Allison stayed in the house only another 4 months and moved out as soon as they could. During those last 4 months that they were still living in that house, Michelle and Allison did not have any more experiences or any interactions with Kenny. Only once or twice after we helped Kenny move on, did Allison have a dream about her dad. For those last 4 months, I was also up there pretty frequently, but not as often as I was right after Kenny died. At no point did I ever feel Kenny's presence again, in that house or otherwise.

Made in United States
North Haven, CT
09 November 2023